MW01135273

Ranch
Ramblings

M.J. Sherman

Illustrated by Betsy Feinberg

Printed in the United States of America

First Printing December 2014
Second Printing July 2015

ISBN 978-1-942573-02-9 Paperback

ISBN 978-1-942574-25-5 Hardcover

Published by: Book Services
www.BookServices.us

Contents

Dedication

This book is dedicated to anyone who has ever dared to live a dream or dared to make the attempt, and to all the neighboring ranching families who supported us in our own dream.

M.J. Sherman

Ranch Life

On days like this, when there's ice on the water tanks, when the wind shrieks like a Scottish banshee, when Mike and I have worked a twelve-hour day, when the nearest town of any size is 60 miles away in any direction — on days like this I find myself wondering, "Why on earth would anyone *choose* to live this crazy life?"

We're up early and out late. We work when there's rain or snow, when it's cold and damp, when the hot sun shines. We slog through mud; we breathe in dust. We shiver in winter, when the north wind howls around our ankles and ears; we sweat in summer when it's 110° in the shade, if we can find any.

There are fences to mend and to build, and hay to haul and gravel to shovel and water hoses to drag around and tanks to fill.

1

Ranch Ramblings

There are cattle to feed and doctor and move and haul and move again.

There are phones to answer and records to keep, meals to make and dishes to do, laundry to wash and cattle to feed. There are errands to run and cattle to feed.

We saddle our horses and ride through the pastures, with cattle to check and some to bring to the pens to be doctored, and fences to check and strays to bring home, and cattle to feed again.

It's a great life! We can quit any time we want to. *After* we've put in our 12 to 14 hours each day!

Up at six, we sometimes work until eight or nine at night. We start in daylight (sometimes) and quit after dark (usually).

Meals are eaten (if we find time to fix them), whenever we can manage.

Everything is long distance, whether it's a trip to town or a visit with the neighbors. We try to do everything in one trip, as efficiently as possible, so that we can get back to our peaceful, bucolic life.

Ranch Life

Out here birds are abundant, the pollen is thick, wildlife surrounds us, and city lights don't exist.

Why would anyone choose this crazy way to live?

Why **wouldn't** they?

It's rich, fulfilling, relaxing, invigorating, restful, hectic, noisy, peaceful, frustrating, frightening, funny, sad, but above all, it's a dream we've found and are living and loving.

Windy Bluffs Ranch

The Cast of Characters:

For seven years we lived on a cattle ranch in Oklahoma. Our small house stood atop a bluff surrounded by 700 acres of native pasture. My husband Mike and I ran the ranch with the help of our youngest son, Josh, who was attending college part time.

For a few of our ranching years, Josh lived in our storm cellar, which was almost as big as the house we lived in. Our house had 400 square feet, with a kitchen, bathroom and living/bed room. It sounds like *very* close living, but since we usually spent 14 to 16 hours a day working outside, it didn't seem all that small. We didn't spend a lot of time in the house. We mostly used it for sleeping and eating, so the size didn't really matter. It was just shelter for us.

Although work was hard and demanding, we also had a lot of fun during those busy years. However tired and toilworn we were, we were never bored!

Several dogs provided us with plenty of entertainment. Three dogs were with us for the entire seven years. Others were with us for varying lengths of time.

Shadow was a mutt that we had acquired many years before we bought the ranch and was probably nine or ten years old when we moved up there. Patch was Josh's three-year-old Dalmatian. Jody was a black lab that we inherited from our oldest son when he and his family moved into an apartment. So we had a variety of breeds and ages of dogs, and a wide range of personalities.

Welcome

Ours was not a traditional cattle ranch. We kept no cows and we grew no crops. What we did was to buy young calves, either steers or bull calves, weighing around 300 pounds and feed them on good native pasture until they had about doubled their weight and were ready to sell for grazing or transfer to a feed lot.

We started out going to cattle sales and buying our own, but that took too much time away from work that needed to be done to prepare the ranch, so we decided we needed help. We asked around, got a recommendation, and hired a buyer named Ralph. Mike went with him the first time or two to show him what we were looking for and then had him start buying on his own.

Ralph went to sales in the three-state area of Oklahoma, Kansas, and Missouri and generally purchased from twenty to fifty head at a time for us. Sometimes he would go to several sales within a day or two and then he would send us larger groups.

When he had a nice cohesive group, he would call us and ask if we could use that many. When we said to go ahead and send them, our *real* work would begin.

The first order of business was to get the holding pens ready. They all had to be cleaned out, the old hay removed, the water tanks cleaned and filled, and the feed troughs dragged into whichever pens were to be used.

Secondly, we had to make sure that we had enough of the required meds and that we had all of the syringes and needles for giving the shots. (We gave all incoming cattle a variety of shots because cattle get sick if you even chance to look at them sideways.)

If we were short of anything, we would have to make a run into town and stock up. This could take anywhere from a few hours to an entire day, depending on the number of animals that were arriving and what we had in stock. We might have to make this expedition once a week — or several times in one week.

The real fun started when the cattle arrived. They were off-loaded into the holding pens; then small groups were run through the alleyway and one by one into a pricey contraption called a squeeze chute. One end of the squeeze chute was opened and the animal was pushed in. The back gate was then slammed shut because if it wasn't closed quickly, the animal backed out faster than he ran in.

As the back gate was closed, the front one was opened just enough for the animal to think he could get out that way. But those gates open inward, and if we judged correctly, we could open it just enough that when he jumped at the opening it would close and have him caught with his head outside and the rest of him inside. BINGO!

The first thing we did was to give everyone their shots and brand them. Then it was on to the other feats of skill.

If the animal came into the chute as a bull calf, he left it as a steer. If he had horns, they were cut (sort of like cutting your hair.) Each animal got a tag in its ear for identification. These tags came in various colors; each individual group got a specific color, and we numbered the tags consecutively. If any animal appeared to be sick, we filled out a "sick card" that held a description of him and what shots he had been given already.

Welcome

When the steer was finished in the squeeze chute, the front gate was opened and he went into a different pen. The sick ones were put in a pen by themselves to make checking on them at a later date easier.

They stayed in the holding pens for a few weeks so that we could determine if they were all healthy and eating well. If they were doing well after a couple of weeks to a month, we ran them out to the pasture to graze and fatten up.

But that wasn't the end of it. Once they had been put out to pasture, we checked on them several times a week. That meant mounting our horses and riding out through the fields, looking at each one if we possibly could.

After a couple of months in the field and about 300 additional pounds, we usually had a good-looking group of cattle to be sold. This welcoming ritual didn't happen just once in a while; we had cattle coming in about as fast as we could get them into the pasture.

Saddle Up?

We spent quite a bit of time in the saddle after we started getting cattle regularly. We had two good working horses that made our job a whole lot faster (relatively speaking) and much easier.

Mike's horse, Joe, was a well-trained cow pony. He was well muscled, not too tall, and raring to go. He was a professional who knew his job and wanted to do it. That meant that *most* of the time he did what was asked of him and did it willingly. But at times he must have been daydreaming about a pretty filly, and then he needed a rap on the head to get his attention.

My horse, Freckles, was *not* a trained cow pony, but he was a good all-round horse. As long as he and Joe were in it together, he'd do almost anything for me. Freckles had a fast easy gait that made him a pleasure to ride for long periods of time.

We fenced off nine acres of real nice grass for the two of them and put up a shelter to protect them from the summer sun and the winter cold.

After about a week in those nine acres, we decided that we had to remedy a problem that was getting worse every day.

Whenever we entered their enclosure to saddle the horses for work, they would start drifting off towards the far end of the pasture. They ignored our calls and other verbal communications, so we had to follow them across the whole pasture and try to corner them to put their halters on.

This was taking up far more time than we could spare, so we came up with a plan. We had to be smarter than they were! We fenced off a small section of their pasture that included their shelter and was close to the entrance gate, put another gate between the large and small sections and dragged in a spare feed bunk. We thus appealed to one of their baser instincts – HUNGER! (Except that in their case it was pure greed).

When we needed them for work, we'd put some oats in a bucket, grab the halters, and the rest was easy. Wherever they were, they'd come running when they heard the oat bucket rattle. Then when they were eating their oats, we'd close the gate between the pasture and the feed area and slip their halters on them. (We really *were* smarter than they were.)

When they were done working we gave them more oats, removed the halters and opened the dividing gate so they were free to run, after they'd eaten, of course!

Fence Me In

When we purchased the ranch, it had a barbed-wire perimeter fence and a set of pipe corrals, consisting of two large pens and some gates. There was nothing else there except native grass and a few gnarled persimmon trees. We divided one large pen into smaller pens with wire and cattle panels, ending up with four smaller pens. We built four or five additional pens and a connecting alleyway next to the pipe corrals to create our holding pens.

We added a squeeze chute and hooked it all together so we could run our future cattle out of one pen, down the alleyway, through the squeeze chute and into a different pen, thus separating the "doctored" cattle from the un-doctored.

Mike and Josh and I put in all of the fences on the ranch by hand. Everything up in the working area and in the pasture we put in with shovels and a post-hole digger. This was not work for the faint-hearted.

We began by digging the holes for the fence posts. Then we set in the T-posts, leveled them, and filled in the holes. When we got to a section where we needed a gate, we had to dig much bigger holes because the gates required much stronger wood posts.

After we had set in a stretch of posts, we had to go back to the beginning of the row and start rolling out the wire. Each side of each pen had five strands of barbed wire. Each strand needed to be stretched tight and hooked to each post. We walked the length of each stretch for each part of the operation. That meant at *least* six trips up and down the fencerow for each side of the fence. Somewhere in each pen we put in a gate; that required a double post on each side of the gate. Those big wooden posts had to be cemented in, so that they would hold the gate without leaning or falling down. (It can be next to impossible to close a leaning gate.)

When we got to the gates with the wire, we had to wrap a double strand of that wire around each post, then cross the wire between each double post and put a cross post between each of the double posts.

All the fence posts, tools, bales of wire, cement bags, buckets of water (no water except ponds in the pastures), and any other equipment we might need had to be loaded onto the trailer, which was hooked up to the pickup. Then we could finally head out for a long hard day of trudging back and forth with lots of heavy equipment.

All of this had to be done before we could begin to even *think* of getting cattle in.

And so passed the first months of our life on the ranch. It was a good foretaste of how we would spend the rest of our time at Windy Bluffs.

Well, Well, Well

Shortly after we decided to build our house, we hired a well driller to come out and drill a well. We had ponds for the cattle in the pastures, but no water for us or for the cattle that would be kept in the holding pens.

The drillers came out and found a very nice aquifer. So we told them, "Gentlemen, start your drilling!"

This was a very small company, but they came well-recommended so we weren't concerned about the small amount of equipment they brought to the job. We didn't really realize just how small they were until they were through with the job.

They started drilling in the beginning of March. Everything was going well. They found good water at about 300 feet. After some discussion, we all agreed that they should drill another 200 feet just to be safe. (An extra hole drilled at the end of the well is called a rat hole.) The water was good and there was plenty of it. We'd be able to keep up with the water needs of all of the incoming steers and our personal use as well.

Now this is where the tale takes a turn. You remember I said that they started drilling in March. Well, March can be kind of iffy weatherwise in Oklahoma. That March turned out to be *very* iffy. The guy running the drilling truck left one day saying he would be back in a day or so for the truck.

We had a cold snap and then a thaw. By this time the truck was sitting in a sizable mud bog. The driller returned, took one look at his truck and said he'd be back when things dried up a bit. This didn't bother us at all, but I found out later that the company had to postpone or cancel several jobs because this was one of only two trucks that they owned. With one of those trucks living temporarily at our place they had to do some major shuffling of their schedule.

Bet you thought this tale was all told, but there's a bit more to add . . .

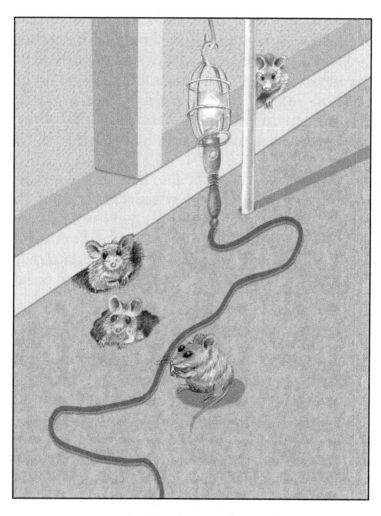

*What we hadn't counted on was a family
of mice that moved into the well house to
shelter from that same howling wind.*

Well, Well, Well

We were a little concerned about the possibility of the pump freezing in the winter. The well house sat on top of a bluff and in the direct line of fire of the north wind, which howled long and loud most winter days and nights.

We thought we had prevented the freezing problem by putting a drop light in the well house right by the piece of pipe that came out of the ground and into the pump. There was just enough heat from the droplight to keep the water from freezing. What we hadn't counted on was a family of mice that moved into the well house to shelter from that same howling wind. Naturally, they didn't enter through the door; they dug a hole under the wall on the *north* side of the building, which, of course, allowed all of that cold air to blow directly on the exposed pipe.

We gave the mice their walking papers, filled the hole, and put hay around the bottom of the building. No more frozen pipes!

Dinner is Served

Even though we turned the steers out into the good grass pasture, those that were out there during the winter months needed some supplemental feed. While they could survive on the grass that was there, we didn't want them just to survive, we wanted them to gain weight.

Because we didn't usually get a lot of snow during the winter, there was always some grass available, but we also took feed to them regularly. The feed consisted of hay and pelleted food.

By the time the cattle were sent to pasture they weighed between 350 and 400 pounds, but they were still young and excitable. (Does that sound like a tale waiting to be told? It is!)

We hauled the big round hay bales to the field on the tractor, put them in the hay rings, and then cut and removed all of the strings that held the bales together. If we didn't remove the strings, the steers would eat them right along with the hay, and there's very little nutrition in binder twine!

If there were steers in the pasture when we took the hay down, we had to beat them off while we got the hay ready. We much preferred doing this task when there weren't a bunch of crazy, excited young steers bouncing around, pushing and shoving to be the first one to the hay bale.

Feeding the pelleted food was an even more interesting affair! We loaded 25-pound bags of feed onto the trailer, gathered up various dogs and any other helpers and headed off to let the games begin.

It didn't take the steers long to figure out that the noisy machine with dogs, bags, and people on it meant *food!* By the time we stopped the tractor and started off-loading feed bags, we already had a bunch of very excited steers in attendance.

We unloaded the bags into the feed bunks in a manner that enabled us to start at each end of the bunk and tear and pour without having to stop to get another bag.

If you think this sounds like a fairly fast and efficient way to get the feed into the bunks, you're forgetting that we were also trying to dodge those excited and very hungry young steers. As soon as the first pellets hit the bunk, they were jockeying for position. We were in their way and they outweighed us by a couple of hundred pounds or more. We quickly learned to push back as firmly as possible! If we weren't fast enough for them, they would start tearing open the bags before we could get to them. Then we'd have to try to pour the food from a torn and sloppy bag, which would slow us down even more.

It was a battle of wits and wills. Who actually won that battle is a moot point, but the cattle got fed and we survived to feed again, so I guess you could call it a draw!

The other job we had while we were out in the pastures during the winter was to open the ponds if they were frozen. Fresh water is more important to healthy cattle than extra food, so we chopped holes in the ice when the ponds were frozen over. We took the sledgehammer and the axe and we chopped until we were out of breath and had enough open area for the steers to get plenty of water.

Dinner is Served

And that was only starters for our day. With all this work accomplished, we could finally get back to our daily chores.

Black and Blue and Washed Away

Our friend Roy asked us if we would like to feed some steers out at his place. He said he had some really good bottomland that fed out good fat cattle.

This wasn't in our plan, but we reluctantly agreed to send fifty head to his place. We had a group ready to go to pasture anyway, so over to Roy's they went.

Now, for those of you who aren't familiar with the term "bottomland:" it means low-lying land, usually along a river, and subject to flooding. I guess we should have thought about this deal a little longer; because — you guessed it — we had a major rainstorm while the cattle were on the bottomland.

Black and Blue and Washed Away

When the water went down enough for us to get to that soggy pasture, we drove out to see how the steers had fared.

Well, they hadn't fared so well. Although we saw a small group stranded on a hill, we didn't see any others, except a few that had fetched up in trees. Cows in trees? Yes, that can happen in a flood. It was a disheartening sight. We drove home and got ready to go in search of the rest of the herd on horseback.

In the end I didn't get to ride out to look for them. Mike took Josh along instead. We, or rather I, had a slight problem while loading the horses.

Joe and Freckles were used to being loaded into the trailer, as we often took them places with us. I said I'd load the horses while Mike got all of the gear loaded.

I got Joe first, because he did better in the front of the trailer. I ran him up the ramp, walked him into the front section of the trailer and tied his halter rope so he would stay there while I closed the dividing gate. I patted him on the butt so that he knew I was going past him; when I got out far enough, I swung the gate out and towards Joe. I told him I was closing the gate

25

and to step ahead so I could latch it. This was usually sufficient to get his attention and get him to step forward.

Well, either Joe didn't hear me, or Mike banged something against the trailer — or Joe was just being ornery. At any rate he suddenly kicked his left hind foot and caught the gate just as I was reaching to latch it. The gate bounced back and caught me right between the eyes. I went flying out the back of the trailer and landed on the gravel driveway just as Mike came around the end of the trailer to get more gear.

He stepped around the back door of the trailer and I landed at his feet. When I opened my eyes and looked up, he had this horrified look on his face. I really think he thought I was dead.

He helped me up, looked at me closely and said he was going to call Josh; I was in no condition to go looking for cattle.

When Josh arrived, he agreed with Mike. I should be sidelined. However, they didn't feel like I should be left at home alone. There were going to be other people out looking for cattle too, and they were going to be using a four-wheeler, so Mike suggested that I ride along with them. The guys finished loading the horses, and Joe behaved just fine.

Mike and Josh rode around and located some of the cattle, but by this time it was getting too late to do anything because of our "slight delay" while loading up. Mike made me promise that I wouldn't risk his reputation by going into town before my two black eyes cleared up, and we got those steers we had located settled out in *our* pasture.

Later that week, after the water had receded, Mike and Josh loaded up the horses again, this time with no problems, and went off to try to locate the rest of the steers.

They had been riding around for half an hour when they got to an area of tall grass. Now when I say tall, I mean that even on horseback, the grass was over their heads. They weren't sure that riding through that grass was going to accomplish anything, but they figured they had to keep looking. After all, those steers had to be *somewhere.*

Just when they were ready to call it quits for the day, Josh stopped and said, "Dad, do you smell that?" They knew that the cattle were very close. They could smell them. They followed the indefinable aroma of wet, muddy cattle and found a big group of them.

Mike and Josh had no idea where they were, so they picked a direction and started herding the cattle that way. They assumed they would eventually find a road or a farm or *something*. They were right. They emerged from the grass and there in front of them were some cattle pens. They were empty, so Josh rode ahead and opened the gate and then came back and helped Mike push the cattle into those pens. They closed the gate behind the cattle and rode to the nearby farmhouse. They explained the situation to the farmer, who replied that they could leave the cattle there. They'd be fine. So the guys went back to the trailer, loaded the horses, and drove home. When they got home, they put the horses up, and I rode along back to start getting the cattle home.

We eventually found 41 of the original 50 head.

It seems we didn't learn our lesson the first time. We sent another group of steers, between 40 and 50 head, out to be pastured somewhere else. And again it was almost a disaster.

Black and Blue and Washed Away

We drove to the property several times to check on the steers. Much to our dismay, they were losing, not gaining, weight, so we loaded them up and brought them home. This took several trips and the last one was a bad one.

Early in our ranching days, we learned from experience that every group of steers contains at least one crazy animal. The last load we brought back from "starvation land" contained *that steer!*

Fortunately, that crackpot steer was one of the last ones off, because he came blasting off of that trailer like a rocket and somehow or another managed to break his leg. We got him back into the trailer, got all of the other steers into a holding pen, and took him to market.

As for the rest of the steers, they went to the feedlot, where they gained more weight than any other group we had ever sent to a feed lot. Much of it was compensatory weight gain, but hey, we weren't concerned about how they gained, only how much, and *they did well!* All's well that ends well.

Ranch Ramblings

Patch and Jody Get Skunked

One day Mike and I were repairing fences in the receiving pens up near the house, and Joshua was changing the oil in the pick-up truck. It was parked on the drive, and Josh was lying under it on the gravel. He would occasionally call for me to bring him a tool or to help him with something.

Josh had just called me for some assistance, and I had started across the drive when he let out a shout, followed by a lot of commotion. Just as I reached the back of the truck, I saw Patch back out from under the truck, only to immediately dive under once more. Josh shouted again. I couldn't figure out what was going on — until I got a whiff of the dog.

It seems that Patch and Jody had chased a skunk into its hole and then tried to dig it out.

They both got sprayed directly in the face. Jody ran off to parts unknown to try to rid herself of the smell.

Patch, on the other hand, ran to Josh for assistance. Since Josh was underneath the truck, she went underneath the truck too! Josh yelled and tried to squirm out from under the truck when she dove under, but that wasn't easy to do on the loose gravel while trying to keep Patch away.

By that time I was at the front of the truck and fully aware of what was happening. I jumped lickety-split into the cab of the truck and closed the door so Patch wouldn't come looking for me to help her. Josh finally managed to wriggle out from under, and he jumped into the cab too. He turned around and gave me such a funny look that I burst out laughing — which got *him* laughing too. Patch was running around and around the truck trying to get in.

Just about then she saw Mike heading over to see what all the commotion was about. I knew I should warn him, but Josh and I were laughing so hard that we couldn't talk. Mike had just leaned down to pet Patch when he got a whiff of her. He jumped back so fast that he lost his balance and almost fell over. In a fit of schadenfreude, Josh and I laughed even harder, out of gratitude that it wasn't *us* outside the truck!

We finally stopped laughing, got out of the truck, unearthed some tomato juice and washed Patch and Jody enough that we could begin to let them get close to us. For several weeks we had a pink and black Dalmatian with a yellow tinged face and a faint perfume of skunk every time she walked past us. Those two never chased a skunk again!

Jody and the Coyote

When we saddled up the horses and rode out to check the cattle in the fields, the dogs loved to go along. They always found interesting things and intriguing smells along the way. They usually stayed within sight or shouting distance of us, and we always enjoyed watching them trotting along with their noses to the ground.

One day we were ambling along on the horses to check on a group of cattle that had been out in the pasture for just a short time. We were discussing which of them we needed to look at first, when I saw Jody take off on a run and disappear around a bluff. Just about then Mike pointed to a coyote trotting along halfway across the field we had just entered.

I mentioned that it looked like the coyote was carrying something in its mouth, probably taking one of the multitude of rabbits that inhabited the ranch home to his family for brunch. We weren't too concerned about it, as there was such an abundance of rabbits that we wouldn't miss a few. As we were talking, we saw the coyote glance behind him and then break into a run. Just as he disappeared behind a small bluff, Jody came into view. She was chasing that coyote! I said to Mike, "That can't be good. I hope she's not dumb enough to get too close to him."

We heard no disturbance, so we went back to discussing the cattle. Right about then we saw the coyote in the distance, running off with his head down. Then Jody popped around the bluff with the rabbit in her mouth!

We stopped in our tracks and stared, dumbfounded. After a minute of stunned silence, we simultaneously burst out laughing. Jody was *not* going to let that coyote steal any of her rabbits! She actually wrested the rabbit away from him and chased him off! She looked so proud of herself when she came back to us with her prize that we couldn't help laughing at her and feeling sorry for that poor hungry coyote family. We never saw her do it again, though she may have tried it more often than we suspected.

Stampede!

Shortly after we bought the ranch, we had a visit from our insurance man. He was going to tell us what kind of insurance we could get on our cattle.

We were working in the holding pens when he arrived, and we showed him the eighty head we had in the pens. They were a fairly good representation of the type of cattle we planned to be purchasing, so we felt that they should be the ones to show him.

Mike and l and the insurance man were standing at the far end of one pen looking across at the cattle in the next pen as they milled around. The insurance man had just started across the empty pen to get a closer look at the steers when we heard a sharp bark. The cattle all shied and started running across the pen towards us. Several strands of barbed wire is not a good way to stop eighty head of panicked, 300-pound steers looking for a place to flee.

Mike and I stood rooted to the spot, thinking, "We just killed the insurance agent. He's going to get trampled by eighty stampeding steers!"

Apparently, Shadow, mostly blind and more than half deaf, had been sniffing around on the far side of the pen that the cattle were in. One of the steers had leaned down to check her out, and its head was only a few inches from Shadow when she suddenly became aware of it. She barked once and ran off, but that was enough to startle the cattle.

We started running across the pen to try to turn the cattle when we saw the agent throw his hands up in the air — he had a clipboard in one hand — and shout once. The steers veered off and continued on around the pen and finally settled down again. By that time Shadow was back sniffing around the pens as if she hadn't caused a major scare only a minute ago. The insurance agent just laughed and assured us that this wasn't the first time this had happened and it wouldn't be the last.

Stampede!

We often talk about the time Shadow tried to kill the insurance agent. Later, in looking over the insurance policy we got on those cattle, we noticed a very interesting clause in the policy. Our cattle were *not* covered if they died in a nuclear explosion, but they *were* covered if they died from a fire resulting from the nuclear explosion!

A Steer Has a Bad Hair Day

We cleaned the water troughs and checked for strings on the hay bales at least once a week. Although we tried to remove all the strings from the hay when we put it in the pens, we usually managed to miss at least one. If we didn't get the strings off, the steers would eat them along with the hay. (They're not the smartest animals in the world!)

Mike was off working elsewhere on the ranch. I walked past one bale with several strings still on it. It would need attention. But first I walked into the pen and started the tank draining. I was about to step over to the hay bale when I noticed a steer whose head had completely disappeared into a deep hole that had been eaten into the bale. I was stepping over to swat him on the butt to move him when he suddenly became aware of me. He jerked his head out of the bale to see if

A Steer Has a Bad Hair Day

When his head came out of that bale, that steer had a full wig of hay perched perfectly on his head.

he needed to run, or if he could just go back to eating.

How I wished I had had my camera with me! When his head came out of that bale, that steer had a full wig of hay perched perfectly on his head. He stood there looking at me with a windblown, spiky wig and a clump of hay sticking out of his mouth, and I just cracked up. A 300-pound red steer with a spiky blond wig and a chaw of hay is a sight to behold. I just stood there laughing, and thinking that even boring chores like cleaning water troughs can be fun if one just looks around a little.

If I hadn't decided to pull strings from the hay bales, I would have missed that steer's "bad hair day."

Tug-of-War

We had another little dog for a while, besides Jody and Shadow. I don't quite know what Ruperick was a mixture of, but he had hair that stood up all over. He looked like he had stuck a paw into an electric outlet. He was kind of black and gray and brown, all mixed together in a way that looked like someone had stirred together salt and pepper and cinnamon. He was cute as could be, but he sure was a pest!

One day when he was just a little pup, he ended up in tight quarters under our porch. Whether he was chasing a rabbit or being chased by one, I'll never know. But he managed to squeeze in under the porch somehow, and he sure couldn't figure out how to get out again.

Josh finally had to pull a slat off of the porch and try to get him to come out that way. Rupe was sure happy to see Josh and ran right over to lick his hand, but he wouldn't crawl through the space that was opened up for him. Josh had to reach in and pull him out. The "jaws of life" operation took some doing and wasted a good bit of working time, but that was Rupe for you.

Rupe was convinced that he was a ranch hand. He was the only one who thought so. He liked to "help" us carry the empty feedbags to the burn pile.

The dogs would usually go to the fields with us when we took feed out to the cattle. Rupe didn't often go out to the fields, but he was always waiting to help us carry the empties when we returned.

We gathered the empty bags and hauled them off, with Rupe stuck to the closest bag. Sometimes he got so excited that he would tug hard enough to pull a bag out of the bundle and run off with it. Sometimes he tugged on his end so hard that the person carrying the bags would be pulled off balance and take a tumble. And sometimes he just got in the way so that we tripped over him and all the bags went flying.

But his very favorite game was to run up behind us, grab the corner of a bag and start tugging on it. Then it was, "Please-oh-please play with me!" He sure was a nuisance!!

Like some human beings I've known, Rupe's way of helping certainly could make a simple job more complicated and time consuming, but made it more fun too! His real assignment was to help us keep perspective, and he sure excelled at that!

The Bone Yard

Our dogs were obsessed with old bones they'd either found or they'd dug up out in the fields. They might come home from their adventures with a single bone or with several. We never worried too much about bone splinters because the bones were always old and weathered.

Over the years our canine family brought us skulls, thighs, shins and shoulders. Sometimes they dragged home sections of spines and once, a piece of spine with an old tattered piece of hide stuck to it. Sometimes there were pieces of bone that we couldn't identify.

One morning we came out of the house to start our workday, and I stopped so abruptly that Mike ran right into me. He asked, perhaps a tad peevishly, why I had stopped, and I replied, "Just look at *that!*" The yard in front of the house was covered end to end with bones. There were enough to build a whole steer, with enough left over to make a small deer!

The bones were scattered around the yard like an out-of-control crop of dandelions. And smack in the middle were the dogs, sitting on their haunches and grinning like they had just found the crown jewels. Those crazy dogs had been very, very busy and it looked like we were going to be too!

Where had they found that many bones? Why on earth did they bring them all home? Who knows? But I was really glad that they were all old and weathered!

It was a while before we got to our chores that day.

The Decapitated Cowboy Hat

Back in the early days, when we were first getting things built and put together, Mike and I were in the holding pens (or what would eventually become the holding pens). We were working by ourselves, separate from each other, stringing barbed wire to divide up the pens.

This was not light work. We had to dig the postholes, pound in the posts, and then string and stretch each of five rows of wire. In the process, we had to unroll the wire, walk it out to the length that was needed and then clip it to the posts, stretching it as tight as possible and then even tighter, as we went along. All without injuring ourselves.

We followed this procedure for each of the five strands, to form six separate pens.

The Decapitated Cowboy Hat

We had been working steadily for several hours when things suddenly began to go wrong. As things began to go from bad to worse, we began to lose our patience and our tempers.

Mike lost his first. He grabbed the straw hat off of his head and threw it as hard as he could. But the hat didn't hit the ground; it flew away from him and sailed like a Frisbee, right through the tightly strung barbed-wire fence.

The crown and brim were sliced apart as neatly as an apple cut in half. There it lay in two pieces, and Mike and I stood there speechless. *We* had survived our work physically unscathed, but the hat! The hat had sustained life-threatening injuries. Once again, after a moment of stunned silence, we both burst out laughing and decided it was time to take a break.

Mike walked over, retrieved the crown, placed it ceremoniously on his head, and marched out of the pen carrying the brim with him like a trophy.

It took us a while to finish that job, but every time Mike would begin to lose his temper I'd go and get that brimless hat and plop it on his head, just to remind him that it's never as bad as it seems at the moment.

The Wandering Goose

We lived far from any town. Our nearest neighbor was a mile away as the crow flies, but it was more like three miles if you went by road.

Being so far out in the boondocks, we were apt to see a lot of wildlife. There were the ever-present rabbits and deer. Our ranch was the main crossroads for several families of coyotes. We had lots of horned toads, which are actually lizards, and various types of snakes, as well as scorpions and other crawly things.

We were also at the very edge of the range of black-tailed jackrabbits, which are actually hares, not rabbits. Though rare in that part of the country, they regularly exhibited their astounding feats of high-jumping and speed on our ranch. Jackrabbits, in moderation, can be an asset to a rancher, as they will eat grasses that

The Wandering Goose

*There, waddling down the lane, oblivious
to any danger, was a goose.*

cattle find unpalatable. Even more important, they will eat plants that are harmful to cattle, reducing poisonous plant cover.

We saw birds of all sizes and shapes, from tiny hummingbirds to northern harriers with a three and a half foot wingspread. We loved the thrumming sound of the harriers as they plummeted at high-speed on their prey. There was even an impersonator, a mockingbird that perched at the top of our tree and convinced us that there were at least a dozen other kinds of birds among the leaves. But the strangest thing we ever saw was the "wandering goose."

I don't remember why, but we had begun to pen the dogs up at night. This turned out to be a stroke of good fortune for the errant Canada goose. I'm pretty certain we'd have had a *dead* goose if the dogs hadn't been penned up.

We woke up one morning to the sound of the dogs barking, not just sporadically, as they usually did, but insistently, without letup. I jumped out of bed and went to the window to see what had set them off so early in the morning. Well, after one look I called Mike over to the window.

There, waddling down the lane, oblivious to any danger, was a goose. Like other cross-country wanderers he'd likely traveled down the Mother Road (Route 66) which was only three miles from the ranch. He ducked under the gate and trundled across the driveway, evidently heading for the pond to the north of the house. Why he was walking there instead of flying in, we have yet to discover. Maybe he couldn't afford to fly, what with ticket prices so high in those days.

When we went out to start working, we found him swimming happily on the pond, so we did not let the dogs out of their pen until we came back in for lunch. By that time, the goose had disappeared. Did he continue to his next destination by foot or by air? We never knew the ending of the story of that lone goose, though for a long time we wondered why he was alone.

Scared to Death

We kept all of our steers in the holding pens for several weeks after their arrival at the ranch. This allowed us to check them for any illness that they might have developed, despite the vaccines we gave them when they first came to us.

There were always a few that got sick, even though we vaccinated them. Any of the steers that didn't respond to the initial round of medication were put in a separate pen so that we could watch them closely and work them as necessary without disturbing the rest of the cattle.

We had one steer in a new group who just wasn't responding to the meds we had provided. We got him up and doctored him daily for three or four days, but he wasn't improving. He only seemed to get worse every day. We finally decided that he was never going to get better, and by now he was costing us more in medicine than we'd ever make on him.

We made the always-difficult decision to put him down. Still, we watched him for several more days. By then he was such a sorry-looking specimen that Mike sent Josh to the house to get the rifle, because that was the fastest and least painful way to put a steer down. The steer was in such bad shape that we were amazed that he was still standing.

Josh came out of the house and as he reached the pen, he cocked the rifle and loaded it. Just as he clicked the rifle shut, the steer fell over dead! Josh was rooted to the spot, dumbfounded, and Mike, with a completely straight face, said, "Josh, I *told* you never to load that thing in front of them." They both burst out laughing. When they had recovered their composure, they dragged the steer to the road for the "used cow dealer" to pick up. Josh walked back to the house, unloaded the rifle, put it and the ammo away, and went back to work.

Of course, the steer didn't actually die of fright. It was just a matter of hours, or possibly a day, until he would have died anyhow. He just happened to die at that exact moment. His timing couldn't have been better, for he turned an unpleasant job into a funny moment.

The Wrong Way Steers

Ralph, our cattle buyer, was really good at his job. Other than one or two crazy animals, he always bought us the quality steers we were looking for.

After Ralph bought what we ordered, he would call to tell us the number of cattle to expect and when Don, the driver, would arrive with the load. Unless he had a full pot load for us, Don often made other deliveries on his way to our place. (A pot load is 42,000 to 52,000 pounds of cattle, which can amount to around 100 calves.)

Ralph bought quite a few of our cattle in Diamond, Missouri. We lived over 60 miles south of there, so Don had quite a drive to get them to us. One afternoon Ralph called with the information on our order, and informed us that Don would be at our place late that evening.

The Wrong Way Steers

We set up and stocked the holding pens and then went about our daily routine. The time for Don to arrive came and passed, and no cattle truck appeared.

Late that night we received a call from Don. He would be in first thing in the morning, and *the cattle were fine.* Our initial alarm abated when we heard Don's story.

He had been deep in a conversation with another buyer when he was handed the envelope with our receipts in it. He just took it and jammed it in his pocket without looking at it. Finishing the conversation, he got in his truck and drove off to deliver the cattle.

The only problem was that when Don left the stockyard, he turned north instead of south. He drove to the ranch and was surprised to find that everything was dark and locked up. By this time it was near 2:00 A.M. He knocked on the door, and when it was opened, he asked a sleepy-looking rancher what he was supposed to do with the cattle. And why weren't the pens ready?

The rancher standing in the doorway replied that he hadn't ordered any cattle. Don said sure he did; he had the receipt for them in his pocket! He pulled them out to show the man and saw *our* name on the envelope!

A sheepish Don apologized and got back in his truck. As he drove out onto the highway he called us and apologized again. He said there had been a mix-up and that after a few hours of sleep, he would get the steers to us.

We finally got the cattle, and we eventually convinced him to tell us what had happened. He finally admitted that he had driven several hours (five and a half, to be exact) north of Diamond, to Monticello, Missouri instead of to us. By then he was far too tired to come all the way south to Windy Bluffs, so he stopped at home to sleep for a couple of hours.

The next time he showed up at the ranch with a load of cattle we had a sign on the gate that said "Welcome to Monticello, Southern Annex." After that incident, if he was late in delivering our cattle, we would ask if he had come by way of Monticello, and he would just laugh and give us our receipts. We never had a load arrive that late again and we always got the best cattle available when Don did our hauling.

No Oats for Freckles

The day started out with no adventure on the horizon, just a light breeze and a pale blue sky. Just like any routine morning, we saddled up our horses and rode out to the pasture to check on the steers. Mike, in his wisdom, thought that doctoring the animals in the pasture was less stressful than bringing them up to the pens, running them through the squeeze chute, and running them back out to the pasture. Less stressful for them maybe, but on this occasion not less stressful for me.

While on horseback we could get up close and get a good look at each one. I guess the animals were dumb enough not to realize that we weren't a natural part of the mix when we were on the horses.

We usually found at least one steer that needed some medicine when we set out, so we always took the supplies in a set of mini-saddlebags that fit over the pommel of my saddle. They were just large enough to hold a bottle of medicine plus several syringes and needles. The medicine we used could be kept in the bags and tolerate being bounced around, so it was ideal for this kind of work.

When we got to the pasture, I filled a syringe and put the cap back on so that when we found a steer that needed doctoring I'd be ready to give it a shot.

On this particular day we set off and rode along, discussing something either important or just plain interesting.

Now these steers had been in the pasture for a while and were considerably larger and heavier than when we had first put them out. They weighed in at probably five-hundred pounds at this point.

As we rode through the herd, we noticed one steer standing by himself, with his head hanging down and his ears drooping forlornly. Well, Mike perked right up and grabbed for his trusty rope. I hung back to keep the steer from dodging off to the side while Mike wound up and threw that ol' lasso right smack around the steer's neck. Perfect throw, first time!

Mike called, "Okay! Just jump off Freckles and give that steer his shot. I'll keep the rope tight."

A single rope around the neck of a five-hundred-pound steer who isn't feeling well and has just been lassoed isn't what I'd call a great idea! But I jumped off of Freckles and dropped his reins.

Cow ponies are trained to stand where they are when the reins are dropped in front of them. Unfortunately for me, Freckles was not actually a trained cow pony, but neither of us foresaw the problem that would cause. I pulled the filled syringe out of the saddlebag and stepped toward the steer. By this time, he was no longer standing quietly with his head down and his ears drooping! He was wild-eyed and frantic, and he was not about to stand there and let me stick that needle into him.

That steer started running, and the only way he could run was side-ways, towards me!

I considered ducking so that the rope wouldn't get me around the neck and strangle me. But then I pictured the hooves of an angry five-hundred-pound steer trampling me and I decided that risking breaking every bone in my body wasn't such a good idea either.

Mike was sitting on his horse Joe, yelling "JUST GIVE HIM THE SHOT!" I shouted back, telling Mike to #>*!??^#!!! By some miracle of dexterity and speed, I did manage to stick the needle into the steer as he went tearing by me. I think I even got most of the medicine into him, but I'm still not sure how much or how I did it. I guess it was my new dance invention: the side-step quick step.

I turned around to mount Freckles before that steer came looking for revenge. Uh oh! Where was Freckles?! He was about three-quarters of the way to the pasture gate. I told Mike he'd better get the rope off that steer and get my #^%%&* horse back here fast because I was not going to walk all the way back to the gate just to let Freckles have his oats.

Mike saw the look on my face, and making no further comment he dashed off and retrieved my so-called cow pony.

No Oats for Freckles

When I had climbed up into the saddle, I told Freckles just what I thought of his behavior. Ignoring my comments, he just sashayed nonchalantly back to the gate and waited for me to open it and let him through. He wanted his oats. HAH!! Not today! We didn't give him any oats, but I'm sure he "shared" Joe's with him.

The Return of the "Bag of Bones"

Like the cat that came back because he just wouldn't stay away, a steer we came to refer to as "Bag of Bones" kept turning up at sale barns and ranches again and again.

We had received our usual load of cattle, probably 20 to 50 head. We had off-loaded them and were getting ready to run them through the squeeze chute when we saw *him;* the "Bag of Bones."

He was the sorriest piece of animal that was ever put on earth. The only thing keeping his bones together was the worst looking hide I've ever seen. He actually creaked when he walked, if walking was what you called his mode of loco-motion.

The Return of the "Bag of Bones"

We managed to get him out of the group and into a pen by himself. We weren't entirely sure he was going to survive the effort of moving from one pen to the next. When we had finished working the rest of the cattle, we *carefully* ran him into our trailer and took him straight to the local sale barn.

Two days later our buyer, Ralph, called and said he had a group of cattle that would fit nicely with the ones Don had recently delivered. Would we be interested? We said sure, even though we hadn't planned on buying any more cattle for a while. Since there were only about 15 or 20, we took them.

Don drove in and backed up to the loading ramp, swung open the back doors of the trailer, and guess who was the first one out? Yup, ol' "Bag of Bones" himself. Don had opened the trailer door and walked to the front of the trailer to push the cattle to get them moving and hadn't seen that tattered and worn piece of cowhide come off the trailer. We called him to the back of the truck, where we were standing and asked him what kind of creature that was that had gotten tangled up with our cattle. He was so surprised that he didn't know what to say at first and then began apologizing, but we stopped him and explained why we were laughing.

Apparently that sorry piece of cow hide had been to every sale barn within 100 miles of us, always mixed in with the healthy cattle and always cut out and sent back.

After a good laugh and a bit of teasing Don offered to take him away, and as we never saw that steer again, we figured Don "took care of him." We occasionally asked him if he had seen our friend Bones when he showed up with a load of cattle, but he always said no.

Baby, It's Cold Inside —

Not all of our stories involved animals. We had one cold, uncomfortable night that neither Mike nor I will ever forget.

The electric lines that fed the ranch were not conveniently located for repairs or replacement. As I mentioned earlier, we lived in the middle of 700 acres, and the electric lines ran across our land and our neighbors' without crossing a single road for about 15 miles. The other problem was that they were abandoned feeder lines from an old power plant and so were fed indirectly from the new plant.

The only way to check the lines was to walk cross-country from one town to the next. That involved climbing over or under the barbed wire of many pasture fences and crossing a whole variety of terrain, *while* avoiding any animals in the area.

Well, the inevitable happened one bitter-cold winter night. Either one of the lines broke or a transformer blew out, but whichever it was, it left us **cold**.

We had a king-sized waterbed that was really too big for our little house. It was really cramped, but it was sure nice to crawl into that bed on a cold winter's night!

That night we crawled into bed feeling rather smug because it was cold and windy outside, and we were warm and toasty inside. At about 2:00 A.M. we both woke up feeling acutely uncomfortable. It took us a few minutes to realize what had awakened us; we were lying on a cold, clammy waterbed mattress.

We grabbed the blankets and moved to the couch and there we finally warmed up enough to go back to sleep. When we woke up again it was 6:00 A.M., and we were only marginally warmer than we had been at 2:00 A.M. It was then that we realized that it wasn't just the mattress that was cold — it was the whole house!

During the night the electricity had gone out. It must have been just after we went to bed if the whole house was that cold already.

To make matters even worse, the only thing we could find to eat was *cold* cereal! Well, you've never seen two people get dressed and out into a truck so fast in your life.

We jumped into the truck, cranked up the heater, and *then* called the electric company and cried, "HELP! NOW!" Then we drove into town to the local restaurant. "Two big mugs of hot chocolate," we ordered. "And keep them coming please!" We had a nice warm breakfast and then went home to do our chores, which we'd have done even if the heat in the house hadn't gone off.

It was almost dark before the lineman showed up to check the lines. He had no idea that he would have to walk out to find the problem and then somehow carry any tools and gear out there with him. Mike offered to take him out in the tractor. It was well after dark when they finally got back and as he was leaving, the lineman said he sure hoped he didn't have to do *that* again soon!

Shortly after that we gave the waterbed to our oldest son and reverted to a regular bed. We still laugh about that mad dash from the bed into whatever clothes we could find, and the unplanned trip into town for a nice hot breakfast. That was the only time we had to deal with a major electrical outage, and we aren't sorry about that at all!

Shadow Vanishes

One blustery day Mike was walking out across the ranch. We usually took the horses when we went out around the pastures, but he had decided to go on foot this time so as to get a closer look at the pastures and fences. When one of us went anywhere on the ranch, one or more of the dogs usually went along.

On this particular day, Shadow was the only one who chose to follow Mike, but as she was old and slow, he was quite a distance away before she managed to get herself moving in the general direction that he had gone. As a result of her late start. Mike didn't know that she had followed him, so he did not keep track of her as he might have otherwise.

Mike made the rounds of the pastures and noted which fences needed mending and which feed troughs had to be stacked until needed. When he had finished his inspection, he came back to the house and said that it felt like it might storm. I agreed and said that I had heard on the news that a bad storm was moving in.

We called the dogs to put them in their pen for the duration of the storm and discovered that Shadow was nowhere to be found. We called and called and walked a ways in the direction that Mike had gone, but we couldn't find her.

A bad winter storm did move in that night and hung around in fits and starts for two days. When we went out after the storm, and there was still no sign of Shadow, we figured she had gone out and gotten lost and died in the storm.

There was little protection out there, except a few hay bales and a few small overhangs in the bluffs. We knew that Shadow probably wouldn't have heard us calling even if she had been nearby. She was so slow that it took her forever just to get from one place to the next, so we were quite sure she was gone.

Late that day while I was out cleaning pens and washing water tanks, I noticed something moving out in the field and wondered if the coyotes were stirring. Imagine my surprise when I looked up a while later and saw Shadow plodding up over the bluff, walking along as if she had just been out for a stroll.

I yelled for Josh and Mike. When I pointed to Shadow, they were as surprised as I had been. We stood there together, watching her meander up to the pen. She went in, walked into the dog-house and slept for two days!

We have no idea how she survived out there in a storm for two days with no food and probably no idea where she was, but she managed to get back in fairly good condition, and seemed just fine when she emerged from the dog house after her two-day "nap."

Patch Falls Off the Truck

Before we built a house at the ranch, we stayed at the house of our friend Ben, who had a farm, but did not live on it. The house was just a few miles from the ranch, so it was a convenient solution to a temporary problem.

We always took the dogs with us in the back of the pick-up. That was before we had Jody, so it was just Patch and Shadow that we had to worry about. Patch could jump into the back of the truck when she felt like it, but sometimes she tried to convince us that it was too high for her to get into. We solved the problem by getting into the truck and starting to drive away. It was amazing how quickly she acquired the capacity to do the impossible, jumping right into the truck with no trouble.

Patch Falls Off the Truck

Shadow, on the other hand, was older and not as tall. She really couldn't get into the truck without a boost. Once in the bed of the truck, she always walked to the front of the truck by the cab. I think she liked that spot because she had less wind blowing on her. Patch, however, wandered around in the bed, side to side and back and forth, smelling all the smells and watching the passing scenery.

We used the truck for many things, one of which was hauling feedbags around. Because we were getting tired of repeatedly opening and closing the tailgate every time we needed to load or unload things, we removed it.

One day we loaded the dogs into the truck and drove over to our ranch as usual. At the end of a long, tiring day, we once again loaded the dogs and headed for "home". We got to the end of the dirt road and turned out onto the highway to drive the three miles or so to Ben's.

I was in the habit of looking back into the bed of the truck to be sure whatever we were hauling didn't bounce off when we were driving around the ranch. We had gone about half a mile down the highway when I glanced back into the truck bed.

I couldn't see Patch, but decided that she must have curled up by the cab for a quick nap. After a moment, I realized that Patch was not in the truck at all. I yelled, "STOP!" Mike pulled over. "What's the matter?" he asked.

"Patch isn't in the truck!"

Mike replied, "She must be lying down up close to the cab." I was certain she wasn't, and we turned around and drove back towards the ranch. And there she was, nonchalantly trotting down the shoulder of the road in the direction of the ranch. We turned around, pulled over in front of her, and helped her into the truck. (This time she deserved a boost.)

When we got to discussing the situation, I remembered that Patch had a habit of standing at the rear of the truck bed when we first started off. She liked to watch things disappear behind the tailgate. She must have been standing there when we pulled out onto the highway and with no tail-gate, she fell off when we accelerated onto the highway. It was a learning experience. After that incident, she always stayed up near the cab with Shadow.

Pot Load Looking for a Home

When it was time to sell our cattle, we abandoned tradition and used a "modern" method that seemed alien to us. We sold our animals over a video auction. This was an excellent decision.

The video auction had several advantages. One advantage was that the steers didn't have to leave the ranch, so they were not put into a stressful situation several times before they were sold. A stressed steer is a sick steer.

The video strategy worked very well. The company would send a rep out with a video camera, and we would get on the horses and just walk the steers back and forth in front of the camera. They didn't mind moving around a bit, and the person who bought them could see more of the cattle than they would with just a quick look at the sale barn.

When the video was run, interested buyers could call their bids in to the auction company. When the cattle were sold, usually by weight, the company would send a truck to the ranch for the cattle. We would drive to the scales with the loaded truck and the cattle would be weighed. The company rep would then give us a check for the amount, according to the total weight of the pot load, and *they* would collect from the buyer. We never had to worry about bad checks or time for checks to clear the bank.

Because we knew the rep, we would usually get detailed information on the cattle and their destination, whether a ranch or a feedlot, as well as the exact location. However, one time the driver didn't even know where the cattle were going. The directions from the buyer were, to say the least, vague.

We had received word that the truck would be in on the following day, so we got the cattle up into the holding pens and had everything ready for loading. We hung around the pens the next day, so as to be immediately available when the truck arrived.

Pot Load Looking for a Home

The cattle hauler came down the road in a cloud of dust. When the truck had backed up to the loading ramp, we started sending steers down the alleyways to be loaded. When the driver was ready to leave, we asked him where these steers were going. He answered, "I don't know! The buyer said I was to head west for two hours and then call him."

We never did hear where that pot load of cattle ended up. We assume they found a home. Or they may be out there still, heading west into the sunset, just looking for a home.

The Bee's House

Our first look at Windy Bluffs revealed nothing more than a perimeter fence and a single pipe corral. In the beginning, we went up to the ranch on weekends. The first time or two we pitched a tent, but the weather got bad, and the tent was not practical. We got very grungy on the weekends and had no way to clean up, so we up-graded to a small used travel trailer. It was weatherproof, and we had a small shower and a flushable toilet! Wonderful!

After we built our small house, we used the trailer for storage, until we built a storage shed and cleaned out the trailer.

The trailer had been sitting empty for about a year, when Josh heard a strange humming as he was working in the nearby garden one day. He paused and sat back on his haunches, trying to figure out what he was hearing. It suddenly dawned on him what it was, and he dove down onto the ground, just as a towering swarm of bees rose up over the edge of the bluff and flew straight into the trailer.

What should we do? We didn't want to leave the bees there to get settled in, but we certainly didn't want to kill essential pollinators. Then Mike remembered that a guy who had worked with him kept bees on his property. We called Tim and asked if he would like to come and retrieve our houseguests. He was thrilled. He had wanted more bees and didn't know where to look for more.

Tim arrived with his gear, including a small bee box, and set to work. We all stopped what we were doing to watch. He had brought along a queen bee, because he wasn't sure he could get to the one in the swarm. He set his queen up in a second little box inside the bee box and put it outside of the trailer. He then proceeded to smoke the trailer.

When the bees had settled down, he closed off the openings around the wild queen and got the swarm into the box with the new queen. Most of them followed, and he sealed up the bee box with the bees inside and drove off with them. That left just a few bees and the wild queen. Much as we hated doing it, we bug-bombed the trailer several times to get rid of any remaining bees or other resident bugs.

Shortly after that, an acquaintance asked if we would consider selling the trailer. We came to an agreement, and the man hitched it up and drove off.

On our trip to town a few days later, we heard a crazy story about this fellow pulling a travel trailer down the road with a swarm of bees pouring out behind it. Apparently, Tim hadn't gotten quite all the bees. Some of them must have been away from the trailer when we bombed it and returned afterwards.

I've always wondered if the trailer ever became bee-free. The buyer never returned the trailer or demanded his money back, so apparently he solved the problem to his satisfaction.

Phones Galore

The house and the storm shelter were built. We now needed more than just a huge cell phone that had to stay in the truck and didn't work all that well.

The lady at the phone company said we could get the phone line hooked up. It would be ready *tomorrow.* We assured her that that was not possible; we needed to get a *line* put in. She insisted that it was just a matter of flipping a switch and that a technician could do it the next day.

We managed to get the number of the technician and explained the situation to him. He looked at his map and said he could put in a line, but it would be about three months before we would have a phone.

We were stunned. We'd gone from being told that we could have the phone the next day to being told that it would be three months! The technician explained that the line would have to come from the north, across the railroad tracks and over the fields to the house. They would need to get written permission from the railroad, as well as the person who owned the land between the railroad and us.

We explained that there was a telephone pole just a half mile down the road from us to the *south* and that we owned the land between the railroad and the house. In addition, we found out that they were going to put in our line from the town of Afton, which would be long distance for all of our contacts. All of our neighbors were on the Vinita line. How was it that if they were all on Vinita, *we* were going to have an Afton line?

After much arguing, we asked to have an engineer come out. When the fellow showed up and we explained the situation, he said to tell the people at the phone company that the house was on the west side of the property and that when the lines were brought in from the *south*, he would come in and run them from there to the house. That way no one would be any the wiser, and we could have the Vinita number.

Phones Galore

The engineer recommended that we put in more than one line to save money. The phone company would run lines in and charge us for putting in the poles and the lines, *unless* we put in multiple phones. It was 3/4 of a mile from the original pole to the house. The phone company would give us 1/4 of a mile of line free per phone. So we had them install three lines, two to the house and one to the storm shelter.

The two lines to the house were for business and personal; the one to the storm shelter we left in for a week and then had it unhooked. (This was done on the advice of the engineer, who said, "You did not hear this from me.") We saved ourselves $5,000 and got our phone lines, despite the runaround from the corporate goofs, in whatever office in whatever big city on some distant coastline. We did laugh a lot about having the only storm shelter in the world with its own private phone line.

FIRE!!

Our ranch sustained lots of native grass because it had never been plowed up and planted. We had some really beautiful grassland for our cattle to graze.

Early each spring, before the new grass sprouted, we would spend a day burning the entire pasture. This kept the weeds down and removed all of the old dead grass that could choke out the new growth. Mike and I usually burned the pasture by ourselves. Sometimes our neighbor would come and help, but it was usually just the two of us.

You can imagine how excited we were when my sisters said they were coming to visit and would be there when we were planning to burn. We told them that we could delay the burn to another day, but they said that they would like the opportunity to help out. It would be an interesting experience. They had no idea what they were getting into!

On the big day, they helped with our usual chores, feeding the cattle and horses and checking the water troughs and hay bales. Then we gathered up our gear, matches, old towels and rags and drinking water and hopped into the pick-up truck, heading to the far corner of the property.

We started by lighting some small, carefully-tended, backfires to keep the main fire contained. (That was what backfires were supposed to do, but it didn't always work out that way!)

While Mike started the backfires, Kris and Beth and I went to the pond and soaked the towels. Wet towels were our most important means of defense against a fire getting completely out of control.

When Mike was ready to start the main fire, we each went to a spot at the edge of the pasture along the fence line and walked along perpendicular to the line of fire. If the flames jumped to an area that shouldn't burn, like the neighbor's field, we beat it out with our wet towels.

Beating out a fast-moving fire with a wet towel is not an easy thing to do. By the end of the day, every muscle in your body hurts. You're covered with soot and smell like smoke. And you're *tired* — bone-weary, feet-dragging, worn-out tired. But when you see what you have accomplished, and see the lush green grass that results, its all worth it.

We managed to keep ahead of the fire and prevent any disasters. Usually we were just beating out a lick of flame that didn't get far, but sometimes it took several of us to beat out tongues of fire that were heading towards the horse pasture or equipment in the field, or the feed troughs stacked by the corner of the fence.

We were just about done when Kris said she had to sit down. Mike and Beth mopped up the last little bit of flame, and Kris and I collapsed beneath a tree and downed about a gallon of water each. I noticed that Kris looked more than just tired; she looked strained too. When I asked why, she admitted she had been really afraid of fire since she was twelve, when she had read a frightening book about a fire. She hadn't wanted to mention it to us, because this was such an interesting experience that she didn't want to miss it.

FIRE!!

Well, that was certainly a proactive way to get over her fear of fire!! Both Kris and Beth said that this was one experience they would never forget.

The cattle did very well on the grass that year. It must have been the wonderful assistance we had when we burned the pasture!

Fishing Opportunity

We had very heavy rains after my sisters visited, and our burned-off pasture grew lush and green. At one point it rained relentlessly for twenty-four hours. We didn't have a rain gauge, but when we came out of the house in the morning we knew we had received a significant amount of rain.

The drive out to the front gate was a gravel road, as was the road out to the highway. Our lane was full of small potholes that were filled with water and so was the road to the highway. We had no idea how much rain we had received until we headed for town that day.

We had a small creek that wandered lazily along the road, sometimes meandering off across a field and occasionally disappearing under the road itself for a bit. At one point the creek got tangled up with the remains of an abandoned beaver dam, but it broke free farther downstream.

There was quite a bit of wildlife that used that noisy little stream. The deer drank from it before dashing off to safety in the nearby woods. The coyotes spied on small game from the tall brush beside it, and the mice and rabbits often stopped by for a quick drink on their way to safety. But by far the most interesting visitor to that busy creek was the resident great blue heron.

We often saw him standing patiently in the stream, waiting for an unsuspecting fish or frog to swim by. He usually fed right there, where the stream slipped quietly under the road. The heron usually came to that particular spot in the morning and just before dark, but after a good rain he might be there most of the day.

After this particular rain, and after slogging through our chores, we headed to town to do errands. We knew that the road out to the highway would be wet, but we hadn't realized how *much* water there actually was until we saw the heron. He was fishing in the middle of the road, standing up to his knees in moving water, grabbing little wiggly, swimming things as fast as he could swallow them.

He was fishing in the middle of the road, standing up to his knees in moving water, grabbing little wiggly, swimming things as fast as he could swallow them.

Fishing Opportunity

He reluctantly stepped off the road to let us pass, and then stepped right back to his spot and continued fishing. He was still there when we returned several hours later, and we laughed, wondering if he would be able to fly back to his nest that evening with his belly so full of good things.

It was several days before we saw him again, and we guessed that he got home and just stayed there until he had digested that smorgasbord of swimming goodies that he had gorged on earlier in the week.

We often talk about the "road fishing" heron and the rainstorm that had turned him into an opportunist. We never had another storm dump that much rain again, and we never saw the heron fishing on the road again.

The Untold Tale

One day, just after lunch, Mike came to me and said that he and Josh were going to saddle up the horses and head out to the north pasture; there was a steer that he wanted to look at again. The last time he and I were out, he thought he had seen a steer that needed doctoring. He took the small saddlebags and the medicine and syringes, in case they found a sick one.

I was cleaning and refilling water tanks, and I didn't need my horse that day, so Josh took him. They rode off to look for the steer, and I went back to work.

I didn't look at the time when they left, but I had cleaned four or five water tanks, pulled strings from several big hay bales, and was laying out hoses to start filling the tanks when I spotted the guys riding to the shed to unsaddle Joe and Freckles.

I finished what I was doing, and Mike and Josh got the horses to their pasture. We met halfway between the house and shed and I asked how it had gone, and had they found the steer? They just nodded and said, "It was fine; we found him; he'll be fine now." They looked at each other and didn't say anything more.

What follows is the story I eventually got from them . . .

Looking Better Than "The Duke"

Earlier in the day Josh and Mike had noticed a steer with a limp. Cattle will often cut the soft bottom of their foot in between their hoofs as they walk through the grass, resulting in an infected foot. Usually we would cut the steer from the herd and bring him up to the pens for doctoring, but today Mike and Josh were feeling like "real" cowboys and thought that they might be able to just rope him and doctor him in the pasture.

Now, roping cattle is not all that hard if you are in a rodeo arena. The animals know to run to the other end of the arena where a gate is their escape from being roped. The arena ground is smooth, the steer runs straight, you go straight, and all you have to do is wait until your horse catches up to the steer and toss the rope over the steer's head. This is not to diminish my appreciation of how skilled a good rodeo cowboy is. They are fast, accurate and lots of fun to watch.

However, in a pasture, roping is a whole different ballgame. The ground is rough and the steer can run in any direction — and usually tries them all. Also, you have to first cut the steer away from the herd so that the other animals don't get in your way. Now cattle are real sociable animals and they usually don't like being singled out because they know that means something bad is going to happen to them. Plus, the cattle can run almost as fast as a horse, so you'd better start your run when you are close to them or you are just not going to get within roping range.

Josh and Mike knew all this, so they eased down into the herd and slowly moved the steer to the edge of the herd and then towards a nice clear area, all the while getting closer and closer to him. Then there was Mike's chance! He spurred Joe and the chase was on. He was right on top of the steer and tossed a perfect loop over his head.

It would have been a perfect pasture roping, except Mr. Steer had one last trick. He cut to the right and before Mike could dally the rope around the saddle horn, the rope was gone from his hand. Lesser cowboys than Josh and Mike would have carried an extra rope. But they felt

95

that would be admitting that they couldn't get a steer with the first one.

So there they were, a long way from the pens, a rope around the steer but not around the saddle, and their pride on the line. The steer stopped just ahead of them in an area of thick brush. The end of the rope was just a few feet away. Now if you are going to be a cowboy, you have to be resourceful and, on occasion, smarter than the cattle. Here was an opportunity. All they had to do was get down from the horses, walk over to that rope and very carefully tie it to one of those bushes. Then they'd have him!

They dismounted and started towards the rope. Before this, they'd never realized what a good judge of distance steers are. They would get within six inches of the rope and that steer would take a step. This is where you have to be smarter than the steer, so they got down on their hands and knees and started towards that rope. The steer took another step. So they dropped to their bellies and very quietly, very slowly worked their way towards the rope. It was at this moment that they simultaneously realized that they were breaking new ground in the art of cowboying. John Wayne had never been seen doing this!

Suddenly Josh had the rope. The steer took off. The steer, the rope, and Josh got all tangled up in the brush. Mike ran over with a syringe of medicine and gave the steer his shot and grabbed the loop. Josh let go. The loop came off the steer's head, and they took a vow of secrecy never to divulge their new technique.

He Came A-Courtin'

Once we got in a group of heifers to fatten up, instead of our usual steers. This was a group that a friend asked us to keep. We treated them just as we did the steers, being paid by weight gain, but we didn't sell them to the auction service as we did the steers.

This worked well at the time because we had only a small group of steers and could keep the herds on opposite sides of the ranch, thus keeping all info and records straight. The heifers were put out in the west pasture, while the steers were kept on east side of the ranch.

As we did with all cattle when we first put them out to pasture, we rode out to check on them almost daily. That way we kept on top of problems that could result in an animal being sent to the "used cow dealer."

He Came A-Courtin'

There was a gate in the fence between our pasture and the neighbor's. That was a good thing, because there was a bull in that pasture.

One morning Mike and Josh rode out to check the heifers, and when they got to the pasture they found an "extra" animal in the pasture. The bull from next door had come to visit.

Mike and Josh set off to cut him out of the herd and send him home. They chased him around the field for a while and finally got him separated from his "harem," only to have him cut back and head for the center of the group. Now, for Mike's horse, Joe, this was just what a day in the pasture was supposed to be: a chance to head 'em up and move 'em out!

They finally got the bull into a corner, at which time Josh dashed down and opened the gate. They then pushed the bull down the fence and through the gate, checked on the heifers, and came back to finish their other ranch chores.

The next day they rode out and found the bull with the heifers again. They chased him around the pasture a couple of times and finally got him back into his own pasture. This continued for several days until one day they rode into the heifers' pasture and the bull looked up at them and started walking over to the gate. Seems he was tired of all the rodeo performances and figured it would just be easier to go home on his own. Josh raced over to open the gate and then he and Mike "escorted" Mr. Bull through the gate.

They never convinced him to stay home, but they did convince him that it was easier to go home quietly than to argue with them.

We eventually sold the heifers and we never saw that old bull in that pasture again.

Steer Jumping

We never knew just what we would find when we got a load of cattle. Sometimes we got a nice workable group of steers, and sometimes we got *the steer from hell.* The tale I'm going to tell you now is about one of the latter.

Our buyer called. Ralph said he had found us a group of cattle that was just the ticket, and they would be at the ranch later that day. We dropped everything else and started setting up the pens for their arrival. We had to be sure that all of the pens had a bale of hay and a full tank of water, and that they were reasonably clean. Then we had to check all of our medicines to be sure that we had enough to vaccinate all the new arrivals. We had to make sure we had all of our tools and equipment in order. And we had to set up the receiving pen.

When the cattle arrived, we had all the gates opened and all of the alleyways between the loading ramp and the holding pen cleared. The only thing we had to do when the driver opened the door was to push those cattle down the alley and into the holding pen.

The only problem was that one of those animals had entered the cattle Olympics and was a pro steer jumper.

We got half of the group into the holding pen, when I noticed one animal charging around the pen with his head up and his ears facing forward. Now, that posture can mean only one thing — TROUBLE! Sure enough, he was getting all of the other animals stirred up and anxious. I called to Mike, "Hold everything! We have to get this guy into a pen by himself before we have a full-blown stampede on our hands." We started to move the troublemaker into a separate pen. We expected him to go through the open gate. He didn't. He went *over the fence* and into the neighbor's field!

We dashed out to head him off at the pass and while several of us were doing that someone else was getting gates and alleyways set up to run him into the proper pen. We got him surrounded and started him moving in the general direction of the ranch. At last, he was moving down the alley and into the pen!

That steer went into the pen all right! Into the pen and right across it, over the fence and into the next pen. About this time we figured out that we had a jumper. We stopped everything and put up another row of fence panels, on top of the existing fence. We figured we had *that* problem solved!

Boy, were we wrong! We pushed him back into the designated pen and turned around to close the gate. When we turned back, we saw his tail disappearing over the extended fence.

At this point our choices were to swear, cry, or find that sucker and show him who was in charge around here! We briefly considered one other solution, but the used cow dealer wasn't due in the neighborhood for a few days. We didn't want that sorry @#*&!@^!# lying around for that amount of time, so we got him back into the reinforced pen and hoped he'd settle down while we finished the task at hand.

We got the rest of the steers off-loaded and settled in the holding pen. The Olympic jumping steer settled down enough that we could go on with our work. As long as he was in a pen by himself, he was reasonably calm. (Calm being the only word available, but not really a correct description of his state of mind.)

We eventually got the other cattle worked and settled in their pen, and then we took the jumper to the local auction house and let someone *else* deal with him.

Permission Granted

We didn't start out with 700 acres of pasture. We started with 310 acres and acquired the rest at a later date. Therein lies a tale.

When we finally got the details worked out with the electric company, they agreed to come out to set up several poles that were needed to bring the electricity from the line a quarter of a mile down the road. They came in along the west side of our lane, which was the boundary of our property at that time.

We started our day in the usual way; we got up, had a quick breakfast, and went out to work cattle and clean pens and water troughs.

When we got to a place where we could quit that for a while, we saddled up the horses and rode out to check the cattle in the pastures. We happened to be up near the house when the power company trucks arrived to begin digging holes and setting poles. We asked if we should stay around, but they said to go on with our work. If they needed anything, they'd find us.

After checking on the cattle in the pastures, we decided to doctor some of the steers in the upper pens. This entailed gathering all of the paraphernalia needed for doctoring.

First we needed the "sick cards," index cards with all the pertinent information on any steer that had been given any medications other than the initial vaccinations they received when they arrived on the ranch. Next, we had to check all meds to be sure we had what we needed and then get the pens set up and open the gates to run the steers into the holding pen.

We were in the midst of all of that when one of the pole-setting crew found us and said that they would need to run a guy-wire off one of the poles. It would have to be placed on the property next to us, and they needed written permission to do that. Mike said that he would go to town and talk to Jim, the man who owned that piece of property. While he was there he would pick up the medicine we needed for the steers.

We knew that we would have no trouble getting permission from Jim, because he was a good friend and our banker, and he liked to help people. Besides, he understood the nuances of ranching, as he had a very large ranch of his own. While Mike drove off to town, I continued to get things prepared for our round of doctoring.

Mike was gone for a long time. In the meantime, I was busy with all the little fussy things that had to be done before a job could be properly completed. I was just starting to get irritated with Mike. I thought to myself, "He's probably in there shooting the breeze with someone while I'm here slogging around **working!**" Then I looked up and saw his truck coming up the drive.

I met him just as he was getting out of the truck to talk to the work crew. I asked if he had gotten permission (knowing full-well that Jim would never say no to that kind of request.) Mike paused and shook his head. I stared at him in total disbelief. "But why not?" I exclaimed. Mike just chuckled and said "I don't need his permission. — *I bought the land.*"

I stood there with my mouth hanging open — and then I told him that he was not allowed to go to town alone any more. Every time he did he bought something!

And that is the tale of how we ended up with over seven hundred acres — and more pastures to work on.

NOT Taking the Bull by the Horns

One of the nice things about living on the ranch was the sense of community. Everyone was ready and willing to help out a neighbor if they needed it. No one said "What should I do?" They just showed up and did the chores that needed doing. Sometimes it was as simple as running an errand or loading feed sacks, but it could be doing all of the feeding of cattle if the owner couldn't. We all simply pitched in and helped, no questions asked.

Our nearest neighbors were an older couple, some of the nicest people I've ever known. One day Ray stopped by the ranch on his way into town to ask if we could help him move his bulls from the bullpen to another pasture. They would be going from the pasture they were in now to one down the road where his cows were.

NOT Taking the Bull by the Horns

We were eager to help and said we'd be there with our horses at the appointed time. The next morning we hurried through our chores, saddled Joe and Freckles, and headed down the road to Ray's house. We had gone just a short distance when we saw him coming over the rise. We hurried ourselves, and we all arrived at the pasture gate at the same time. Thus began our adventure.

We opened the gate and rode around behind the bulls to start them moving. Once we had them on the move, I headed out the gate and onto the road to discourage those six enormous animals from turning towards the main road and to stop any cars that might approach.

Everything appeared to be going well, and the first big bull stepped out of the gate and onto the road. He hesitated, looked over at Freckles and me standing in the road and decided that he'd be nice and go the other way. (If he had chosen to come my way, I'm not sure if I would have argued with him *or* his buddies who had just joined him on the road.)

The guys followed them out and Ray went on past them to lead the cattle down the road and provide a deterrent to their going beyond the final destination. After the last bull was on the move, I fell in beside Mike and we kept those guys moving in Ray's direction.

They were moving along at a slow but steady walk, when the last one in line stopped. Mike and I stopped too and sat quietly while the big guy looked around and tried to decide if he should follow his buddies or go back to the pasture he had just walked out of. Or maybe he could make a break for it and head off on an adventure.

At this point Joe, Mike's cow pony, decided that it was *his* job to move that animal. So he hunkered down, swiveled his ears forward and prepared to do what he was trained to do — ***work cattle!***

Mike suddenly realized what Joe was getting ready to do and he leaned forward and rapped him on top of the head to get his attention. Then Mike proceeded to explain to him that although Joe was indeed a marvelous cow pony, this guy out-weighed him by at *least* a thousand pounds and it probably wasn't a good idea to make him angry! Joe paused, considered what Mike had said, and after a moment of consideration decided to proceed with caution.

Joe and Freckles stepped slowly forward, and I guess the bull decided he was outnumbered.

He turned and followed his pals on toward all those waiting cows.

That was one experience I'm glad I had, but not one I'd like to do again. A two-ton animal with horns walking toward you, however slowly, is utterly intimidating.

SOLD!

After seven years things had changed, the cattle market looked iffy, and we had an empty nest, so we decided to sell the ranch. We decided to sell by auction, because we weren't interested in waiting for a buyer to come along.

Everything was sold at that auction — and I mean everything. If it wasn't moving, it got sold.

Once the auction was announced, a day was set aside for people to come and see what was being auctioned off.

Shortly after we bought the ranch, we had a shed built to hold the feed bags and horse tack and tools and miscellaneous orphaned items we had no other place for. One elderly lady came out on viewing day and as soon as she saw that shed, decided that it was a sine qua non, i.e. something absolutely essential in her life.

The shed was still solid and had been well built, but lets face it, it was seven years old. It had been used hard and was showing its age.

That elderly lady was one of the first ones there on sale day, and she bid on a few things. Then the shed came up for sale. Well, she was determined she was going to get that shed. And get it she did, but she paid more for it than she would have paid for a brand new one, and on top of that, she had to pay someone to come and move it to her place. We couldn't figure out why *that* shed was so important, but if she wanted to pay that much for it, well it was her money.

There were two other such crazy bids, which proved my earlier statement: If it wasn't moving it got sold.

There was exceptionally active bidding going on for our junk pile. Now why would anyone *pay* to go through a junk pile? But they did, and for the rest of the day they dug through it like kids looking for buried treasure.

We also had some lively bidding on two buckets of scrap metal, things like bent horseshoe nails and rusted barbed wire spikes and old broken fencing tools. I don't understand — but I guess the buyers were happy.

I miss the ranch, but we've found a new place with a big sky where we can see the stars at night and watch the sun go down to the horizon — the Sonoran Desert.

CPSIA information can be obtained
at www.ICGtesting.com
Printed in the USA
BVOW06s1818200217
476690BV00015B/147/P